Blessings
Eva McCall

Lucy's Recipes
for Mountain Living

Lucy's Recipes for Mountain Living

Eva McCall & Emma Edsall

Illustrated by Anthony Fair

Historical Images
Fairview, North Carolina

Text © 2002 Eva M. McCall and Emma C. Edsall
Illustrations © 2002 Bright Mountain Books, Inc.

Historical Images is an imprint of Bright Mountain Books, Inc.

Printed in the United States of America

ISBN: 0-914875-39-6

Recipes have been neither kitchen tested nor taste tested; experiment and enjoy at your own risk. The authors welcome your comments. They may be reached at grannylucyrecipes@yahoo.com.

Recipe for Living in the Southern Appalachians

First, you will need to be creative in order to survive in the mountains. Then, you will need a good amount of ambition to carry out your creative endeavors. Next, sprinkle generously with humor. This will keep you going when the creativity and ambition are a little on the slow side.

Blend in a few drops of honesty to help you stay on the straight and narrow when all the above looks like it's going to fail. And don't forget the generosity, the courage, and more than a dab of stubbornness.

Douse with a good dose of sincerity and compassion served on a daily basis to your fellow mountaineer, and we'll promise you that after baking for a few seasons in the Appalachian mountain sunshine, there's no other place you'd rather be.

Contents

Introduction

This book is intended to be for recreational reading only. We have neither tested nor tasted the recipes. Inspired by watching the first contestants on "Survivor" try to spit roast a rat, we have simply collected and retold "survival" recipes and stories from our grandmother, Lucy Davenport Carpenter, and company. She married our grandpa who had already fathered thirteen children, and together they had four sons. Lucy was a remarkable woman. If you haven't already done so, you can read about her role as wife and mother in Eva's books, *Edge of Heaven* and *Children of the Mountain*.

This book shows another side of Lucy's daily life: raising, gathering, growing, and cooking food for her hungry family. Since we didn't inherit carefully typed-out recipes to pass along, we've tried to recall what we watched her do to achieve those unforgettable flavors. We both contributed and signed the memories which introduce each chapter, and we recalled family events and recipes individually or as a team.

Growing up in the Appalachian Mountains was hard in Lucy's time. Can you imagine living in a time when there were no electric lights or indoor plumbing?. . . when clothes were beaten over a wash bench, then boiled in a big, black pot, and scrubbed on a washboard? . . . when every bite you put into your mouth was eked out of the hard mountain clay? . . . when the only toys children had to play with were homemade or were old, broken dishes and discarded clothes used to play house? But the lessons we learned from Lucy are the lessons we taught our children, and the tradition lives on and on, forever.

—Eva McCall & Emma Edsall

Fireplace Cooking

The fireplace was the heart of the home in Lucy's time. The family gathered there after a long day's work or school and enjoyed food and story-telling. Some of the best snacks were roasted there as the stories were traded, and when the food was ready, they'd sit back, enjoy the snack and reflect on what had been told. Many of the snacks came from trees, some from the ground, some were seasonal. All these bring back memories of that time, sitting around the fireplace with the light from the fire shining on those young faces.

~ ~ ~

After hearing all our lives about how the family enjoyed roasted chestnuts, my husband decided to try some. Getting the chestnuts wasn't a problem; we had a tree in the front yard. What we didn't have was a fireplace to roast them in. I didn't real-ize that he'd filled a baking sheet and put them in the oven until I heard the oven exploding. I opened the door and chestnuts came at me like bullets. Now we know one important thing: Don't try this without putting a hole in the shell of the nut first. This was one important fact that was not passed down.

—Eva

Hoe Cakes

On the mountain, hoes are not only used for gardening or killing snakes. As soon as the crops were gathered in and there was no more use for the hoe outside, Holman would have the boys clean up a couple for family use around the fireplace during the winter. In wintertime, it wasn't unusual for the chores to be done by lantern light. Since it got dark so early, Lucy liked to have supper over early, but this meant the children would be hungry before bedtime. She'd mix up a batch of her cornbread without as much liquid, and they'd pour it onto the hoe and hold it over the fire until it was done—thus the term "hoe cakes." Of course there was fresh butter and plenty of homemade syrup to go along with it.

Hot Ash-roasted Potatoes

The hoe cakes weren't the only treat waiting for the hard-working group of children. Buried deep in a hot bed of coals were a big pile of Irish potatoes. When the hoe cakes were eaten, someone would use the hoe or the poker to uncover the potatoes. Usually another print of butter was needed. And don't forget the salt!

Chestnuts Roasting by the Fire

The hardest thing about roasting chestnuts by the fire is digging them out of those awful burrs they grow in. Holman's boys would stomp them out and the nuts were buried in the hot ashes to bake just like the potatoes.

Chinquapins

By the time a good heavy frost caused the chinquapins to burst from their burrs, the children of the mountain were ready to sit around the fire and pick the tiny morsels from their shell. Many a cold night was spent eating these nuts and telling haint stories. The hardest part about enjoying a snack of chinquapins is the gathering. They can't be picked until after the frost has opened the burr, but preferably before they fall to the ground or it will be hard to find the tiny, dark nuts. Another challenge is finding them before the squirrels do. They love to stash them away for the coming cold weather just as the children did. There were enough children to remember where they'd stored their supply, but I still wonder how those little squirrels remember.

Dried Apple Pies

The minute the Carpenter young-uns smelled Lucy's dried apples cooking, they knew they were in for a treat. She'd save some of her cathead biscuit dough, roll it thin, and spread it with the cooked fruit. Sometimes if she had spices she'd add a few. This was folded in half and sealed, using a fork to press the edges together. The big iron skillet was set on a grate over the fireplace and the pies fried in butter. These were enjoyed with a glass of cold, sweet milk. There's nothing better to bring sweet dreams.

Popcorn

On nights when there weren't hoe cakes or roasted potatoes, there was plenty of popcorn. Some of the children would shell the knobby little ears while the others took turns shaking the popcorn in an old-fashioned popcorn popper over the open flame. Once again the butter was needed. Poor cow, she never knew she was worth a fortune.

Roasted Marshmallows

Marshmallows roasted over an open flame were something that the children in *Edge of Heaven* weren't lucky enough to have, but the young-uns in *Children of the Mountain* were able to enjoy this treat occasionally. Marshmallows were bought during the holidays and the children didn't have to be told to round up a stick for roasting the soft candy over a bed of hot coals.

Beans, Taters, and Other Fixin's

Taters were a mainstay of my childhood diet. I know because even after years of education and city living, nothing comforts me when I'm sick like a bowl of potato soup. I remember walking the furrows behind Daddy as he and the mule labored to dig straight ditches in the hard clay, dropping the one-eyed potato pieces, then stepping on them to ensure they "stuck." That was spring. The fall brought the digging. If we had a large enough patch, sometimes Daddy and the mule plowed them out, and we followed along picking and sacking up the newly turned potatoes.

At twenty-one and a new college graduate, I ventured out of the mountains to see the ocean for the first time. On that trip I saw the little children in eastern North Carolina following the tractor-pulled plow and planting tobacco by hand. I felt a kinship with them I've never felt with my professional peers.

—Emma

Hominy

The winter was long and cold, and fresh food was hard to come by. When Holman saw Lucy searching the canned goods for a fresh taste, he'd bundle up the young-uns, light a lantern, and head on out to the barn loft for some story-telling and corn shelling, so Lucy could make hominy, which she especially prized. The lantern vied with the moon to cast the longest shadows as they approached the door to the barn loft. Martha, the littlest one, whined and hid her head in his shoulder at the strange sight. Once inside, the older ones lit more lanterns, pulled some corn out of the corn crib, and shelled the kernels off in rows as they listened to Holman tell about marrying Mary, his first wife, and coming to the mountain. The chills would wear off as they listened to stories of their ma's and pa's younger days, and the horses and cows added their voices to the children's.

Some nights our Uncle George would come by and join in the storytelling with tales of the Spanish-American War. He loved to boast of going off to fight the "furiners." And he'd try to show off by using some of the Spanish he heard. "Si, Holman, si," he'd croak in his little high-pitched voice. Unfortunately, Uncle George didn't quite get the pronunciation down pat and it always came out "Sigh, Holman, sigh!"

Lucy used the shelled corn to make hominy. First she soaked the dried kernels in a big pot of water with hickory ashes she had tied up in cheesecloth and placed in the top of the pot. Then she dumped the liquid off the kernels and cooked it for days in her smaller three-legged cast iron pot on the back of the stove. We don't remember any bacon, fatback, or other seasonings in the hominy, but it wouldn't be surprising to find we've missed an ingredient or two.

Fried Taters and Ramps

Spring finally crept up Carpenter Mountain. The younguns looked with disgust at the remaining potatoes whose long antennas reached toward any sunlight that happened to filter through the cracks of their bin. Hattie wanted to know if they could dump them in the sinkhole since they were too shriveled up to eat. Lucy told her no, there were still some good meals left, and what they didn't eat would be planted. Hattie wrinkled up her nose in protest, complaining that nothing that looked that bad could taste good.

Lucy picked up an empty feed sack and took the child by the hand. She told her what they needed to make the potatoes edible were some ramps. The two set off in search of a good meal. Lucy explained to Hattie that ramps belong to the onion family and would spice up the wilted potatoes. She told her how her pa said that the early settlers called them "ramsen," and later it was shortened to ramps.

Lucy swore to Hattie that they were a good spring tonic, and that her ma used them to treat coughs and colds and made poultices from the juice of the strong summer bulbs to stop the pain and itching of bee stings. Soon Lucy found one of the plants and showed Hattie the lily-of-the-valley-like leaf. Calling Hattie to follow, Lucy went around the hill to a big patch of ramps that blanketed the ground. As they stuffed the feed-sack full, she told Hattie that by the time the trees leafed out and shaded the ground, the ramps' leaves would wither and die, leaving only a single bud on a naked stalk. She broke open one of the leaves and sniffed the strong garlic-like odor. Hattie turned a sorrowful face toward Lucy and asked if that was why her sister Annie May died. Lucy hugged Hattie tight and explained how, just like the ramps, life is a cycle. They hurried down the mountain and while Lucy peeled the lifeless potatoes and sliced them paper-thin, Hattie washed the mountain dirt from the bulbs they had collected and tore away the light, protective skin.

Lucy diced the ramps up with the potatoes. When they were mixed thoroughly, she dumped them into a skillet of hot bacon grease. The aroma drifted through the door, beckoning to every hungry Carpenter who was within smelling distance. It wasn't long until they swarmed the kitchen, fighting for a taste of withered potatoes and ramps. As an extra treat, Lucy crumbled up some bacon and sprinkled it over the top.

Potato Soup and Dumplings

The smell of freshly plowed earth and cow manure filled Lucy's nostrils as she plodded up the hill to where Holman and the young-uns were planting potatoes. Hattie threw something into the grass. Lucy picked up the shriveled potato and approached the family, chastising them about wasting good food. Lucy peeled away the wrinkled skin, exposing withered but sound potato. Cutting it into chunks, she dropped it into a pail, instructing the young-uns on how to cut out the eyes where the new sprouts grow. The young-uns could plant those, leaving the rest of the potato for dinner.

When the pail was full, Holman asked one of the boys to carry it to the house for her. After several washings to remove the red clay, the potatoes were put in a big pot with enough water to cover them and set on the stove to boil. A heaping cup of chopped onion or a few ramps were added for flavor. As soon as they were soft enough to stick a fork into, there was a good dose of salt and pepper added. Then came more liquid—chicken broth if she had any—and a generous amount of cream and butter. This mixture was left simmering until Lucy heard her family washing up out at the branch, then she mixed up a large batch of her biscuit dough, brought the mixture to a rolling boil, and dropped in the tiny squeezed-off dumplings. The hungry family crowded around the table as Lucy ladled a large portion onto each plate. Hattie took a bite and wanted to know how the potatoes were brought back to life. Everyone laughed. Holman assured her there was nothing Lucy couldn't accomplish when it came to food.

New Potatoes

Hattie loved to be the first young-un Lucy trusted with her special fork. This was the fork used to "gravel" for new potatoes, and Hattie loved new potatoes. She didn't even mind scratching out enough for the rest of the family as long as she got to pick out the special ones just for her. By early spring, Hattie could hardly wait for the potatoes they had planted only a few weeks ago, because she was good and tired of the potatoes Holman had carefully stored away in the cellar, which were now old and tough.

She carried a big bucket along with the fork out to the garden just about the time the tender, young plants finished blooming. She had to get down on the ground and up under the plant, then gently scratch the dirt away from the surface of the new potato. The taters ranged in size from marbles to walnuts. Anything bigger than a walnut was left to grow. Once she had her bucket full, she carefully carried it out to the back porch where Lucy would wash the tiny morsels and scrape them with the backside of a case knife to remove the tissue-like paper skin. Lucy boiled the potatoes until they were just barely soft enough to stick a fork into (not her special gravelin' fork). If the new potatoes were not parboiled first, it was said they would give us "the trots."

She dumped the water into the slop bucket and placed the potatoes in a big frying pan of hot bacon drippings. She loaded them with salt and pepper and popped them into the oven to brown. These delicacies were served with freshly churned butter.

Salad Peas

One of the first crops to go into the ground after the potatoes was salad peas. Today they're called snow peas, the kind used in Chinese food. Our mother picked them when the pea inside was still small. She'd pull off the strings and snap them in the same way as a string bean. She'd slow-cook them for about half the day with some of the new graveled potatoes and season with butter. Sure not the way the Chinese cook them!

Fried Summer Squash

There's nothing better than a good mess of fried summer squash. Lucy knew this and didn't waste any time picking the squash soon after they'd shed their blossoms. She knew if they weren't picked within a day or so of the flower dropping off, they'd become too tough. After a good washing in cold spring water, she'd slice thinly and coat with a mixture of flour, cornmeal, salt and pepper, and a dash of sugar. She'd fry the squash in leftover bacon grease until brown and crisp, and serve with some of her famous cornbread.

Field Corn

Can you imagine a world without sweet corn? Well, the children of the mountain didn't have any. Our Dad planted sweet corn for us, but he hadn't grown up with it. Lucy would pick field corn when it was still tender and clip off the kernels, scrape the cob, add a little sugar, salt and pepper, a good portion of butter, and cook it in the frying pan for about fifteen minutes.

Mater Biscuits

The Carpenter young-uns would fight over Lucy's leftover biscuits, especially if there were ripe tomatoes. They'd rush out to the tomato patch and gather several of the ripest ones. After washing, they'd slice them into nice, thick pieces. After salting a slice to taste, they'd slide it into a cut biscuit. They were also a favorite for a packed dinner, either for school or when out working the new ground. As for the name, mountaineers are known for calling potatoes "taters," and tomatoes "maters." Sounds good to me.

Pinto Beans

Cooking pinto beans was a daylong task on the old wood stove. Actually it started the night before with sorting, washing, and soaking the dried beans. A little baking soda was added to the soaking water to keep the beans from giving us too much gas. As soon as the fire was stoked up in the morning, the bean pot was set on the back of the stove and the beans proceeded to cook till suppertime. When the beans started to warm up, Lucy would cut a big hunk of fatback brought in from the smokehouse and throw it in the pot to flavor the beans.

Along about sundown, when the shadows would start lengthening over the mountains, but before the menfolk got home, Lucy would put on a cake of cornbread.

Potato Cakes

Potatoes were a staple for the mountain people, even when it looked like they had died and needed to be dumped into Hattie's sinkhole. This was also true with any leftover cooked potatoes. In Lucy's household there weren't many times when there were leftover mashed potatoes, but when it happened, she'd stir them up with a few eggs, some chopped onion, and a little extra salt and pepper. Enough flour was added to make a good stiff dough. These were squeezed out into small biscuits and fried in a good helping of bacon grease. They were usually eaten at breakfast along with eggs and bacon or sausage.

Breads

Bread, like potatoes, was a staple for the children of the mountain. When vegetables or meat ran low, Lucy would make more bread. This tradition carried down to my family. There were five children, my mother, my father, and of course, Granny Lucy. It took a twenty-five-pound sack of flour to feed us for a week. I remember the time my dad decided it would be cheaper to buy "light bread." That's what we called store-bought bread. In the late forties, a twenty-five-pound bag of flour would cost $2.50. Bread was ten cents a loaf. Dad came home with twenty-five loaves of bread. We thought we'd died and gone to heaven with all that fresh, soft bread ready to eat any time we wanted it. Well, that "any time we wanted it" was what got us in trouble. By Wednesday all the bread was gone and there was no flour. It was cornbread the rest of the week, even for breakfast. Dad never tried that again. Sometimes if he had the money, there would be store-bought bread and peanut butter for lunches, but generally it was biscuits with whatever Mother could find to put between them.

—Eva

Cathead Biscuits

Now there's nothing better than a pan of Lucy's cathead biscuits along with butter and homemade syrup or jelly. Holman thought Lucy's biscuits looked just like the heads of the barn cats! She had so many to cook for that she didn't always have time to roll out her biscuit dough, although she'd usually roll them if there was company.

Lucy would fill a large mixing bowl with flour. In the center, she'd make a nice little hole and dish out a handful of lard to put in the hole. To this she added some salt, baking powder, and if she was using buttermilk, a little baking soda. This was mixed with flour until it was the texture of coarse salt. Adding a little buttermilk or sweet milk, she'd begin to work in more flour. When it became good squeezing texture, she'd place her thumb and forefinger in a circle around the dough and pinch off a biscuit. The pinching process was something no one but Lucy seemed to conquer.

Cornbread

Lucy's cornbread was a staple she used almost daily raising her large family. What else would fill up all those stomachs?

Many a night, after a long day's hunt for bear, deer, turkey, or squirrel, Holman and his sons would come home and sit down to a supper of hot cornbread, beans, and cold milk or buttermilk.

Today, if we wanted cornbread, most of us would pick up a box of cornbread mix at the local market. Not Lucy! For one thing, the local market was about fifteen miles away from their home on Carpenter Mountain. Her preparations for cornbread started with the first corn shucking; she was right there picking out the "cream of the crop" to be taken to the gristmill and ground into cornmeal. Once the selection was made, Lucy's evenings were spent sitting by the fire and hand-shelling the corn.

It wasn't an uncommon sight for the neighbors to see Lucy riding the old gray mule bareback down the mountain to the mill, with a sack of corn slung in front of her. She'd stay and visit with Joe Hastings, the mill operator, until her meal was ground, and then make her way home.

Usually Lucy would have buttermilk and an egg to go in the bread, but many times these ingredients were missing, and she'd do like most mountain women and make do with what she had.

Here is Lucy's recipe, more or less. Remember, her cooking wasn't an exact science. It was always a dab of this and a dash of that.

First, the cast iron skillet should be preheated on a wood-burning stove until hot. Cover the bottom of the skillet with bacon drippings, then sprinkle with dry cornmeal, and let it brown. Take the pan off the heat and mix about one cup of cornmeal with a half cup of all-purpose flour. To the dry ingredients, add one-and-a-half teaspoons baking powder and one-quarter teaspoon soda. Stir in two tablespoons of oil or bacon grease. Add one fresh egg from the hen house and enough just-churned buttermilk to make the mixture the consistency of pancake batter. This consistency is important. Lucy discovered the thinner her mixture the more moist her cornbread. Make sure the pan is hot and dump the mixture in, then bake at four-fifty until golden brown. Sometimes it was hard to get the wood-burning oven that hot.

One last reminder, if there's a crowd of people at dinner like Lucy had to cook for every day, this recipe can be multiplied by ten.

Hogs

I've heard that pigs are one of the cleanest and smartest creatures. After slopping the hogs and cleaning the sty, I, for one, can understand why pork is not "kosher." But it was a mainstay in our diet until well after Granny Lucy died. As a young child, I loved it. I can remember my eagerness for fresh fried liver on a hot biscuit. Now I no longer like liver and really don't care much for pork at all.

However, my family loves country ham biscuits on Christmas morning. Christmas is about the only time I serve country ham. My son was fifteen before I cooked it at all, and then only because his girlfriend (now his wife) was coming to breakfast and it was one of the few meats she would eat.

Speaking of which, it is wise for me to remember that my tastes changed, not only with age, but also with the availability of choices. Killing the hogs was not sport, but survival. I don't remember Granny Lucy being overweight. It's much too easy to pop into the store and pick up a package of plastic-wrapped, pre-processed, and sometimes even pre-cooked meat for dinner.

Many of our weight loss diets today call to "eat only when you're hungry." I'll bet that if we all had to kill and dress our own meats we would be only too willing to do so.

—Emma

When I was a little girl, my favorite time of year was hog-killing time. My mouth waters when I think

about the smell of backbones and ribs cooking.
Lucy knew how much I loved them, so she'd make
a point of having a pot boiling when I got home
from school. All she did was boil them and season
with salt and pepper.

After we'd had our fill, she'd can the leftovers
for winter. I was always amazed when she'd open a
jar and heat it without adding a drop of water or
stock. The juice they were canned in made its own
gravy.

I think most of the fun came from fishing the
tasty morsels of meat from the bones. It's sort of
like we do now when we eat crab legs—all that
work for those tiny bites of good, sweet seafood!

—Eva

There were seventeen of them. Not seventeen young-
uns, but seventeen squirming, squealing piglets. They were
all healthy except for one. She was the last to arrive in the
world, the last to the supper table. By the time she'd wiggled
her way there, the table was all filled. Her brothers and
sisters were much bigger and not about to share.

Lucy watched as she tried, time after time, to squeeze
into the maze of pink little bodies, each time getting shoved
away. By morning this little one would be dead, if not from
starvation, then from smothering. She scooped her up and
carried her to the house in her apron, warmed some milk
and dipped her fingers into it. The pig didn't waste any time
sucking the drops. This process was continued until the
little grunts subsided, then she wrapped her in a old ragged
quilt and placed her in a box behind the stove.

Soon the little pig that hadn't stood a chance had free
run of Lucy's kitchen. As she went about her daily chores,
the pig was right behind. By the time hog-killing time rolled
around, she was a candidate for bacon, but Lucy couldn't

stand the thought of "her pig" sizzling in the frying pan. Holman always kept a few for breeding. As he made his selection, Lucy's pig—sow, by now—never left her side. It was as though she knew Lucy would save her from the frying pan. As Holman pointed with his cane to the hogs to be slaughtered, Lucy untied her apron and dropped it over her sow. Holman's cane stopped at the apron, then moved on. She guessed he'd realized if he wanted bacon from her kitchen, he'd need to let her sow become a mama.

Preserving Hog Meat

After Holman killed hogs, the job of preserving the meat for the winter was the next big job. Today we'd take a hog, if we had one, to the slaughterhouse and have it killed, cut up, and packaged in neat little bundles with the name of the cut stamped in red letters. We'd bring it home and store it in our freezer until we wanted to cook some, then we'd take out a package, thaw in the refrigerator overnight, and cook.

Holman tried to get his meat into the smokehouse immediately after slaughtering. Sometimes it would still be warm. If twenty-four hours elapsed, the blowflies would already be laying their eggs. The cold weather kept the meat from spoiling. Some liked to just salt it down, but not Holman. He'd mix his salt with some molasses, black and red pepper, and coat the meat. The amount of time he left this mixture on depended on how cold the weather stayed. If any of the meat made it to spring without being eaten or spoiled, he'd wash it and coat it with brown sugar and pepper, and hang it in a clean white sack until "Mr. Hard Times" came along.

Hog Jowls and Black-eyed Peas

Come New Year's Day, Lucy would always have a pot of black-eyed peas cooking on the stove. This was a mountain tradition and it was a superstition that for every pea eaten, we'd receive a dollar in the coming year. You can bet there was a lot of pea eating going on at the Carpenter house.

To help flavor the peas Lucy'd drop in part of a hog jowl she'd convinced Holman to cure just for the purpose of cooking with peas, beans, and greens. As for the superstition, well, we don't know how many dollars were present at the Carpenter house the next year, but we do know that none of them starved.

Slab Bacon

The bacon Lucy fried in *Edge of Heaven* was store bought. Most years Holman cured his own bacon by salting down the side meat of the hogs he killed in the fall. In good years he had enough to feed the family till spring, but not the first year that Lucy came to live with the family.

The hardest part of having bacon wasn't the cooking, it was trudging out to the smokehouse in the cold, pulling down the sack, cutting off the bacon needed for that morning, putting the sack back up, and trudging home, and all before the sun came up. The salty side meat was tasty but hard to carve as it was cured with the skin still on the outside.

The secret to frying good bacon is a hot pan. Lucy always put the cast iron skillet on the stove first thing and tested it with a drop of water before she started the bacon sizzling. Once she started, the aroma wafted through the kitchen, living room, up the stairs, and even out the door. When these smells reached the barn, Holman knew he'd better hurry in from the feeding if he wanted any bacon for breakfast.

Old-fashioned bacon didn't stick to the pan while it was frying like many of the store-bought brands of today will because it had no additives.

The Rest of the Hog

Mountain people never wasted anything, especially hog meat. They knew all too well that when hard times came knocking at their door, they wouldn't be too proud to slice off a chunk of tongue that had been scraped, boiled in salt water, and canned. Most will say there's nothing better than a pot of stew made from the tail, feet, ears, heart, and nose. These were boiled and any vegetables they had handy were added.

From the minute Holman began the process of cutting up the hogs he'd killed, Lucy was right there with every empty pot and pan that she could find. She'd scrape all the fat from the hams, middlins', shoulders, and even the entrails. The fat was left outside all night to get cold. The next morning it would be firm enough to cut in egg-size lumps to put into the big, black wash pot to boil. Lucy always said adding a pinch of soda would keep the cracklins' from smelling while they cooked and from tasting strong later. She'd add enough water to keep them from burning and cook it slow, all day.

Stirring was Lucy's job. She didn't trust any of the young-uns around a pot of hot grease. By nightfall, she'd dip off all the grease (lard) and put it into buckets. The lard was used for cooking and soap making. At the bottom of the pot was the leftovers called cracklins'. She saved these to make cornbread, and there wasn't anything Holman loved more than a good mess of cracklin' bread on a cold winter's night.

Lucy loved to bake the pigskin and serve to the young-uns as a treat. Today we call it pork rinds and buy it in the junk food section of the grocery store.

Holman liked hog brains scrambled with eggs. With hot water, Lucy would loosen the thin layer of skin covering the brain. She'd boil them with salt and pepper to taste, then mash them with a potato masher. She'd crack several fresh hen eggs and add a good portion of the smashed brains, then scramble in some of her hot bacon grease. Maybe the taste of bacon overpowered the taste of brains and made them edible.

The liver—what good eating! It was one of our favorites, especially when dredged in flour with lots of salt and pepper and fried fresh from the hog's belly. Some mountain people made "liver pudding" or "liver mush." They'd boil the liver in salt water until tender and run it through a colander, making a fine paste. The meat was then mixed with some of the broth and brought to a slow boil, then thickened with cornmeal. It was seasoned to taste with salt, pepper, sage, and red pepper. It was then molded and let set until cold, then sliced and eaten like we eat lunch meat. This was not one of Lucy's favorites and therefore the family never developed a taste for it.

The lights (also known as the lungs) were sometimes boiled down until there wasn't any water left and they were the consistency of gravy. They were mashed and served the same day, as they could not be saved. Think I'll pass on this one, but I will put my order in for some of that sausage Lucy used to make. She'd round up all the lean scraps not used any other way and run it through a sausage grinder. Coarse salt was then added with all the brown sugar she could spare and a good helping of black pepper. Sage was always a must, but used sparingly since it is a powerful spice. Red pepper gave it color as well as making it warm to the taste. Lucy would roast her homegrown red peppers in front of the fire and crush them for her sausage and souse meat.

Storing the sausage was never a problem with so many young-uns to feed, but Lucy made sure there was enough to pack in clean intestines and hang in the smokehouse to cure. Sometimes she'd pack corn husks full, then tie and hang. Later, when jars and lids were more plentiful, she'd brown the sausage balls and pack her jars about two thirds full, pour hot grease over them, and turn them upside down to seal. The jars were stored upside down.

The hog-killing season wouldn't be complete until Lucy made a good-sized batch of "souse meat" or "headcheese," as some called it. After the head was harvested, Lucy would boil the whole head. Of course, this didn't happen until she'd soaked it in her washtub to get the blood out. When the head was well cooked, it was allowed to cool, then all free hands set about picking the meat from the bone. It was run through the grinder, and just like the sausage, it was seasoned to taste with sage, red pepper, black pepper, salt, garlic, and a little cornmeal. Some put in onion and vinegar. After it was thoroughly mixed, it was stored in the smoke-house so the winter weather would keep it fresh.

They ate the intestines also! These were called chitlins. This was one job that Lucy didn't hesitate to let that bunch of young-uns do. She'd have them carry the tub of insides down to the branch and wash them clean. Some were used for stuffing sausage. The rest were put into jars of salt water and allowed to sit for three or four days, then taken out and rinsed well. In the winter, they can be salted and stored in jars for a few days before cooking. To cook, Lucy would dip them in a batter of flour, water, baking powder, and some-times an egg, then roll in cornmeal and fry in hot bacon grease. Another treat for a crew of hungry young-uns!

Now we can put the hog to rest, or at least his bones, for that was just about all that was left when the Carpenter bunch finished with him. Oh—one more little detail and that's the bladder. What in the world can you do with a hog bladder? It's not too hard to figure out if you think about what the hog uses it for, or at least it wasn't for our brother. His favorite water gun, probably his only one, was the blad-der from a hog.

Green Things

Is it any wonder these tough, hardworking, mountaineers liked a lot of greens in their diets? They instinctively knew that to stay healthy these were needed. Many of them had either experienced themselves or heard stories of how their native country, Ireland, had suffered famine. Even little green leprechauns are part of the heritage and still have a place today. And how about the four-leaf clover? As a child I spent many a day searching for the little green leaf that had four leaves instead of three, knowing this would bring me some of the Irish good luck for sure.

~ ~ ~

I was reminded of Lucy's fried cabbage when my husband and I went to an excellent restaurant in Michigan to celebrate our anniversary. I ordered their roast pork with dressing. The waiter asked if I would like the house specialty, grilled cabbage. Being a lover of this vegetable prepared in any way, I said yes. When it was served, I recognized it as something Granny Lucy had made when I was a child.

There are some differences in the way Lucy made it and the way I now prepare it for my family. All I do is go to the local grocery store and select a nice, firm head of cabbage. Lucy took a sharp butcher knife and went to the garden. If it were wintertime, she'd take her hoe and dig one out of the bank of dirt where they'd been stored. Once the cabbage had been harvested, or in my case,

purchased at the market, it is washed and shredded. I use my electric shredder. Lucy used her sharp
butcher knife. Lucy fried bacon nice and crisp and
crumbled it into bits. I use prepared bacon bits. Lucy
used the hot bacon grease to fry the cabbage. I use
non-saturated fat to saute my cabbage. Lucy added
a good portion of sugar along with salt and pepper,
seasoning to just the right taste. I add a teaspoon of
sugar with my salt and pepper, reasoning that sugar
isn't good for me. Lucy cooked the cabbage until it
was slightly browned, then served with the crumbled bacon bits. I cook until wilted, telling myself that
vegetables shouldn't be overcooked, then top with
artificial bacon bits.

The cabbage can be prepared my way or Lucy's,
but I must say, for all my grandmother's unhealthy
cooking habits, she lived to be eighty-eight or
eighty-nine years old. My grandfather was in his
eighties. Even with all my so-called healthy ways of
living, I doubt if I outlive either of them.

—Eva

Cabbage Greens

By the time the early cabbages began to head, Lucy was
so hungry for a mess of cabbage greens she'd pick off the
large green leaves to cook. The young-uns used to say that
this left the cabbage head as naked as a jaybird.

Lucy didn't have to worry about spraying like we would
today. When the worms decided they wanted a meal of
something green, be it cabbage or tomatoes, they'd seek out
some leaves and begin to chew. As soon as evening arrived
but before it was too dark to see, Lucy would head to the
garden with her flour sifter and a good amount of flour.
After a good dusting and heavy dew, the next morning the
poor little worms found themselves baked in place.

Well, the cabbage might have been naked and the worms baked, but as soon as Lucy washed the leaves nice and clean, they were ready to boil, along with a good-sized chunk of fatback. After they were cooked, she'd coarsely chop up the leaves (and meat) and bake a pan of cornbread. Once again the Carpenters ate like kings and queens.

Stewed Cabbage

Now believe it or not, Lucy's naked cabbage grew to be nice big heads. Just as soon as they were firm but before they began to crack open, she'd pick one or two, depending on how many she was feeding that meal. She'd quarter it and put it in a large pot with some water, salt, pepper, and a great big scoop of lard, boiling until done. When it came time to eat, they'd all forgotten the naked jaybird that used to stand in the garden.

Sometimes if Lucy happened to have a ham bone that had been gnawed clean, she'd boil it first, then lift it out and add the cabbage to the ham water. This seasoned the cabbage and gave it more flavor. Other times she'd add vegetables, depending on the kind that was available.

Creasy Greens (Turkey Mustard)

Lucy taught the young-uns to watch for tiny turkey foot-shaped leaves called creasy greens or turkey mustard as they played along the sides of the branches. They were easy to identify, and she encouraged the rivalry between them to see who could bring home the most, knowing it would take a great big portion for them all to get a taste. Lucy didn't boil or fry these! They were actually eaten raw—sort of.

Lucy let the young-uns pick the greens, but she assumed the role of watchman in looking over each leaf for bugs or worms. She washed the leaves carefully and set them aside to drain. Right before eating, she dumped a good helping of hot bacon grease over them to wilt the leaves. She ate her greens with onions or ramps if she had them, and cornbread. If there were enough, she even let Holman and the young-uns have some!

Dandelion Greens

Picking dandelion greens might not seem like a big deal since they're everywhere, but the weeds have to be picked before the famous little yellow flower blooms. Lucy knew that if she waited for the flowers, the greens wouldn't be tender. She also knew she had to look for brightly colored leaves with no wilting or brown spots. She soon learned the paler the leaf, the more tender the taste, and these were especially good to eat as a salad, while the larger dark ones were good for cooking.

Like other greens, dandelions need to be thoroughly cleaned to remove any dirt or soil. Submerge in water and rinse and repeat until the water runs clear. Parboil and drain, then fry in hot grease. Of course, Lucy used hot bacon grease.

Lucy used these greens as a decongestant or spring tonic, and she'd heard her ma say many a time they'd take the swelling out of the feet.

Fried Greens

The summers were long, hot, and filled with fresh food from Lucy's garden. Once the beans, beets, tomatoes, and potatoes were pulled, gathered, sorted, skinned, washed, cooked, dried, or canned, Lucy scattered her fertile garden with tiny little seeds saved from the mustard and turnip plants grown the previous year. By late September, the ground was again beginning to green with new plants. These were a welcome change from the foods of summer. Mixing the milder-flavored turnip greens with the strong-flavored mustard toned the mustard down. Lucy didn't much care for the turnips themselves, but the young-uns loved to gnaw on raw ones, sprinkled with some salt. The pigs just loved 'em, too!

Lucy went out to the garden early in the morning, while the plants were still wet with dew, and picked at least a bushel basket full of the greens. Many mornings she was dripping wet when she met Holman coming in from milking. If the weather was nice, she boiled the greens outside to keep the strong odor out of the house. But if need be, she hung her pot over the fire in the fireplace, or set it on the back of the stove, and after meticulously looking at and washing the front and back of each little leaf, she would boil them. Lucy believed in cooking things until they were dead. Today, we'd probably just wilt the leaves in hot water, but if the water wasn't green when she drained it from the leaves, Lucy would cook them some more. After draining, she dumped the greens in a hot frying pan of bacon drippings, salted and peppered them, then fried them for supper.

Fried Green Tomatoes

From the minute Lucy planted her tomatoes, Holman's mouth began to water for a good mess of fried green tomatoes. As soon as the vines lost their blossoms and the young fruit started to form, he began his watch. If Lucy caught him eyeing a good-sized tomato, she'd remind him of her rule—no one touched her tomatoes until she got a nice red one. It didn't take too long after the first ripe one was picked until Holman would show up in her kitchen with his hands full of green ones.

First, Lucy would remove the stems and slice the tomatoes, then dish out cornmeal, flour, salt, and pepper to coat them. Once each piece had a good dose of the mixture, she'd fry them in a pan of hot bacon grease. It's a good thing that all of that bunch didn't like this recipe, because it wasn't until late summer that there would be enough to feed a whole crowd. Now, I know that tomatoes are green before they're red, but remember, Lucy liked *her* tomatoes red!

Granny's Cabbage Salad (Coleslaw)

Start with one good firm cabbage, bald like Lucy's. Cut it up in a large dishpan, along with one small onion, and then take a cabbage chopper to it. (Our mother's cabbage chopper was a tin can with the lid removed and the tin sharpened.) Chop until no longer coarse. Dice up and add a red tomato or two. For the dressing, nowadays we would use mayonnaise, but Lucy used clabbered milk because she didn't have mayonnaise. To the mayonnaise add four or five tablespoons of sugar with salt and pepper to taste, and enough buttermilk to make the mayonnaise the consistency of dressing. There's not a better salad, and I'm sure Lucy's family was just as happy with her mayonnaise-free dressing. As the saying goes, "you never miss what you never had."

In later years, Lucy did learn how to make a version of today's mayonnaise. She'd beat three eggs, adding a little sugar along with a cup of cream. She'd add half a cup of vinegar very slowly and cook in a double boiler until thick, add salt to taste, and mix well. This made about a pint of dressing, but it took all of it for a batch of Lucy's coleslaw.

Poke Salad

The minute spring started to creep up the mountains, Lucy and the young-uns could be seen scurrying around fencerows, roadsides, barnyards, pastures, and especially the new cleared ground in search of the tender sprouts of poke-weed. After a long, cold winter without any fresh vegetables,

Lucy could hardly wait to harvest the new shoots. Besides, waiting too long would run the risk of getting sprouts that were poisonous. Her ma had educated her on the when, why, and how of eating this plant. She'd said never pick the leaves once they are too tough to snap with the touch of your fingers. The root and big leaves are very poisonous.

Before the hunt began, Lucy corralled the young-uns and gave them instructions. The last thing she said was to pick it all because Holman would clear the pastures and barnyard of any remaining plants. Although animals won't eat pokeweed if there's anything else to eat, Holman didn't want to run the risk. As soon as he'd let Lucy pick what she wanted, he'd have the young-uns out destroying it, leaving only the plants that animals couldn't get to. Those were left to bear berries that could be used for wine or dye.

After harvesting, the leaves were looked through for bugs and worms, then washed and placed in the large iron pot, and boiled until the water turned green. That water was drained and the greens were boiled again. This process was continued until the boiling water looked clear. The greens were drained and dumped into hot bacon grease and cooked some more. Sometimes for variety, Lucy would whip up several eggs to cook with the greens. This not only gave them a different flavor, but also fed more people, which was always an important element at the Carpenter house.

Wilted Lettuce

By the time the leaf lettuce got big enough to pick, Lucy knew if she didn't wilt it, the hot summer sun would. She'd pick a dishpan full and look for bugs, then wash well. She fried up a good batch of bacon grease, added a little vinegar and sugar, and poured it over the lettuce and young onions. Crumbled-up bacon sprinkled on top made it extra good.

Wild Game

In *Children of the Mountain,* Lucy doesn't eat beef, and even buries a cow rather than cook it. It will come as no surprise that there are no pot roast or meatloaf recipes in this book. Some people remember the Kennedy days as Camelot. I remember my first hamburger, the first beef I'd ever tasted. It was a lot like the McDonald's hamburger (the small one) and it cost fifteen cents at a grill in the back of a local department store. To this day, I swear the onions are the best part of a burger! As a youngster I was introduced to some unique proteins. My daughter refused to eat at the Chinese restaurant until I assured her that all the food was American—just spiced with a few spices and herbs she wasn't used to. Now she loves Beef and Broccoli! All the meats in this section are strictly American—and the spices, too.

—Emma

Nowadays people are not the only ones doing the hunting. With the growth of the bear population and the lack of food, the bears are also hunting. In the spring when they come out of hibernation, they're hungry and come down into cities looking for food. Beehives, garbage cans, and bird feeders are being robbed, causing quite a disturbance with neighbors.

I had an experience with this, firsthand, a few summers ago. I was tucked away in our mountain cabin with my computer. Stories of bear invasion were reported daily. I saw some bear droppings in the yard and asked my niece if bears came through screens. She laughed and said no. That night a loud noise woke me from a sound sleep. I looked out the window to see a screen flying across the yard. As I stepped through the door leading to the porch, a big, black bear greeted me. He was half-in, half-out of the window with what looked like a smile on his face. I stomped my foot and slapped my leg and ordered him off my porch. He backed out, but in the process he fell backward. As I gazed down at what appeared to be a six-foot bear, I couldn't help but think about Lucy. I realized I was truly her grand-daughter for she, also, would have stood her ground.

—Eva

Baked Black Bear

Start with one large black bear, dead. How to kill the bear is a matter of personal preference, but try to avoid using a shotgun, as it's nigh unto impossible to extract all those little pellets with a dull knife.

Not normally being grain fed, bear tends to be a bit on the strong side, kind of a wild taste, Lucy used to say. Generally, she'd soak it in a bit of vinegar to tone it down a mite, and then she'd bake it in the oven of that old wood cook stove. Lucy believed the longer the meat baked, the better. Helped to tender it up, she said. I don't remember it being too tender, mostly just dark and stringy, but it was a nice change from the salt-cured pork in the smokehouse.

In Lucy's day, bear hunting was a community activity. As soon as the bear season opened, the men began to gather at Holman's with musket over shoulder and bear dog in tow. As they tromped off up the mountain, Lucy knew she wouldn't see them again until they'd killed two or three bears or the season ended.

Bear hunting, like so many other things, has changed. Men still go hunting but usually not as a community group. They'd just as soon not drag a bear home and face the prospect of butchering and cooking it themselves as not too many wives still enjoy cooking exotic meats.

Squirrel and Gravy

Some people shy away from eating rodents, but it's hard to beat a good mess of squirrel and gravy in the fall. You eat the squirrel just like fried chicken and serve the gravy over baked, hot, white sweet potatoes.

Lucy parboiled the squirrel. Even a little thing like a squirrel can be mighty tough if it's just grilled or fried. She saved the drippings from the morning bacon or fatback to fry the squirrel. After it boiled until tender, she'd mix salt and pepper with flour and toss the squirrel in the mixture, then dump into the hot fat and fry until brown on both sides. Removing the squirrel, she'd add three tablespoons of flour and stir constantly over low heat until the mixture was thickened and flour was browned, but not burned, add one-and-a-half cups of liquid (stock from the pot where the squirrel was parboiled) and stir until the gravy was thickened.

If Lucy had any broth left, she'd mix up a batch of biscuit dough and drop it by the tablespoon into the boiling broth to make squirrel dumplings. After all, filling all those bellies at supper took more than a few skinny squirrels.

Cottontail Rabbit

After the first few frosts had turned the leaves to brilliant reds, oranges, browns, yellows, and even some purples, the rabbit hunt at the Carpenter house was on. The reason they're not hunted until cold weather is they have worms called wolves, and it takes cold weather to kill the worms. These little pests are also found in cattle and squirrels.

The Carpenter boys liked to gut their rabbits when they got home in the evening, while some of the neighbors preferred to do it on the spot. One short slash in the belly, the same way the backbone runs, provided an opening to remove the entrails. The hide wasn't removed until it was time to cook or there would be a whole family of blowflies living in the meat.

Once the guts were removed, Arthur would cut across the middle of the rabbit's back. He'd insert his fingers and pull both ways. The coat would slide from the rabbit, and he'd take out the feet in the same way as he would a squirrel's. He never cut up the rabbit. This was left up to Lucy because she insisted it be cut her special way. She'd separate the ribs and back by cutting the sides up and down. The legs were removed also. Just like the squirrel, she'd parboil in salt water to make it tender. For frying she'd place the rabbit parts, seasoned with pepper and salt, into hot bacon grease and brown. Sometimes she'd coat them with meal or flour before frying.

If she didn't want to mess around with frying, she'd dip the pieces in a mixture of one egg, five tablespoons flour, a little milk and pepper, and bake in the oven until brown.

Her family loved it when she took the time to cook up a mess of her famous rabbit stew. She'd simmer the rabbit in salted water until tender and add onion, potatoes, and carrots. Sometimes small dumplings were dropped in to stretch the stew even further.

Fried Trout

Mountain trout are best when they're not too big. Eight to ten inches is just about the right size. Catching the fish was probably the best part of having trout. Lucy would fry up a bunch for breakfast every Sunday morning after fishing all day on Saturday. The young-uns got to clean the fish. Scraping gills and guts was something I learned not to shy away from at an early age. I would sharpen the knife on the whetstone well before starting because once I started gutting the fish, I didn't want to cut my hand in all that fish slime.

Hold the fish by the gills, near the head end, and insert a knife in the bottom of the belly close to the tail, and slit it right down the middle. A sharp knife will lay that baby wide open. I'd slip in my hand and slide out the guts. The cats love 'em. I would also scrape down the sides once I finished cleaning out the insides. This gets all the sharp little gills and any slime off the fish before the cooking.

Lucy would roll each trout in a mixture of half cornmeal and half flour, sprinkle generously with salt and black pepper, then dump it in a frying pan of bubbling hot lard until it was brown and crisp on each side. Uncle George loved Lucy's fried fish. He'd sit down at the table, pile up a whole plate of those little trout and cornbread, then proceed to eat the fish—heads, bones, and all—then chase it with a big mouthful of cornbread.

Lucy's Hush Puppies

Fish fries were a way of life for the mountain people. All the neighbors knew Lucy to be the expert when it came to making hush puppies. Even Hattie admired her skills. When one of the neighbors gave Hattie a hound puppy, she named him Hush Puppy.

As soon as the menfolk brought in the first catch of Brookies and Browns, Lucy would dish out a good portion of cornmeal, then she'd add a little flour to smooth out the texture, throw in a pinch of soda and salt, an egg, and mix with fresh churned buttermilk until it was moist enough to form into two-inch balls. Knowing that some of the young-uns would make a fuss about the onions, she'd scoop out enough to make an onion-free batch, and then cut up a good-sized one in the remaining batter. When this was done, she'd fry them in about two inches of bacon drippings and drain on a brown paper sack. Yum-yum, finger-licking good!

Home-Fried Frog Legs

Frog legs were one of Holman's favorite wild meats. Lucy left the gigging and cleaning up to the menfolk. After they'd dressed and cleaned the hind legs and threw the rest away, they took them to the kitchen. Lucy had a pan of grease ready. By ready, I mean it wasn't too hot. Not hot like for deep-frying potatoes or fish. If it were too hot the legs would jump out when they were dropped in. First thing after having the grease the right temperature, she'd stir up a mixture of flour, salt, and pepper and roll the legs in the mixture. Sometimes for something different, she'd whip up an egg in buttermilk, dip in the legs one at a time, and then roll in breadcrumbs.

Turtle at Its Best

First, we'll have to do what Lucy's boys did and find a good big mud turtle. They're the kind for eating. After locating a good-sized one, the first problem is chopping off the head. Harley was an expert at this. He'd hold a stick in front of the turtle. Angry at being teased, it would stick out its head and bite the stick, and then Harley would simply cut it off. He'd select the easy method of removing the shell by dropping the turtle, shell and all, into boiling hot water.

He'd then cut the meat loose from the shell, gut it, and cut into small chunks. Harley also used the meat from the legs to help feed such a large bunch, but most people only use the meat under the shell.

Just because Harley had harvested the turtle meat didn't mean he'd be eating it that night. After it reached Lucy's kitchen, she soaked it overnight in salty water to remove the wild, strong taste. The next day, she'd parboil it. While it was boiling, she'd mix together a cup of plain sifted flour, a teaspoon salt, a little baking powder, two eggs, and one-half cup of milk. Draining the parboiled meat, she'd let it cool and then dip into her mixture and deep fry until golden brown.

Sometimes for variety, she'd stew the meat in sweet milk (what they called milk straight from the cow), butter, pepper, salt, and eat like oyster stew.

Another method of cleaning is to skin the turtle by cutting off the bottom plate first. Then cut between the meat and the domed shell and gut it. Cut off the legs and discard them, if you choose not to use this meat. By the time you reach this stage, if you still have an appetite for turtle, proceed to cook it. Quite honestly, we recommend buying turtle meat already removed from its shell!

Makin' Do

Growing up in the mountains to me means making do. To this day, I get more pleasure out of making do than I do going out and purchasing what I need. Recently, my daughter and I were stripping wallpaper and needed a tool. She said, "I'll just run to the hardware store and get what we need."

I said, "Why don't you run to the kitchen and get us a couple of pancake turners?" They worked great, and we not only saved money, we saved time.

~ ~ ~

It's been more years than I like to think about since I attended beauty college in Flint, Michigan. Before we were allowed to work on real live women, we had to complete a number of hours of textbook work. When the instructor said that the next day's lesson would be on bleaching, I was mortified. Being from the mountains where even cutting a woman's hair would send her straight to hell, let alone coloring, which was a sure-fire hell ticket, I didn't know what to think.

The only bleaching I was acquainted with was Lucy's bleached apples. Every fall she'd peel a whole passel and slice them thinly, placing them in a five-gallon wood tub. A little bit of sulphur was placed in a container, lit with a match, and set in with the apples. The tub was then covered with a clean, white cloth. This process was repeated several times. Some people with big tubs lit the sulphur for three or four days before they took out the apples and stored them in another container. The result was white apple slices. The sulphur had taken out all the color. They were used for pies or applesauce.

My biggest concern with the hair bleaching was how were they gonna get the head, attached to the body, into a tub to light the sulphur. I attended class, praying all the time that I wouldn't be selected as the model. I need not have worried. Someone who did this process on a regular basis had volunteered. Instead of finding a wooden tub at the workstation, I found a client with a plastic cape wrapped around her, hair parted, and an instructor poised with an applicator bottle in her hand. Inside was a white mixture. As she began to explain the process, I raised my hand and asked if it contained sulphur. I was assured that the bottle only contained peroxide and powdered bleach. I still think that powdery stuff was sulphur because when the instructor had finished, the results were the same: white apples, white hair.

—Eva

Sassafras Jelly

After Lucy made herself a cup of sassafras tea by boiling the roots for half an hour and straining, she'd measure two cups of tea into a pan and add about four cups of honey (without honeycomb). She'd then put some of the dried sassafras root and bark into a dishtowel and beat with a hammer until it was a fine powder. This was mixed in and simmered for several minutes. This made a good syrup-like jelly to serve over any fried cake.

Drying Better than Frying

There was always a lot of frying going on in the Carpenter house. Well, in the fall there was always a lot of drying going on also. Bushels of apples were peeled, cored, sliced, or cut in rings. The sliced ones were put on a board, and the rings were placed on a broomstick. If the sun was shining, they were put outside to dry; if it was cloudy, they were placed in front of the fireplace until brown and rubbery in texture. The whole process depended on the amount of heat. When dry, they were stored in flour sacks until time to cook. They were used for dried apple stack cake, applesauce, and fried apple pies. So even the drying found its way to the frying pan.

Leather Britches

Lucy knew that in the dead of winter Holman would be wishing she hadn't canned so many green beans, so she used the last picking of green beans to make leather britches. She'd clean them and sometimes break and lay them on cardboard in the sun to dry. Other times she'd let the young-uns use a needle and thread and make a string of beans. These were hung on the clothesline so as not to touch anything until they were dry.

When they were ready, she'd store them in a clean flour sack and hang it in the can cellar with the other food. The very minute Holman said, "I think I'll skip the beans tonight," was the night Lucy put on a mess of leather britches to soak. The next morning, she'd put them on to cook with a chunk of fatback from the smokehouse. By suppertime, Holman's mouth would be watering for a bite of the light-colored beans.

To make leather britches the modern way, plant or buy green beans that don't have strings. Dry them in a dehydrator and store them in a plastic bag in the freezer. They'll be pretty much like Lucy's, but don't be surprised if your family isn't all that appreciative.

Persimmon Butter

After the first frost, the Carpenter children gathered the wild persimmons that grew in abundance on the hillsides. They'd carry them home and Lucy would make her grand-mother's persimmon butter. To about a gallon of cooked persimmons she'd add a quart of buttermilk and a little soda. They were then run through a colander and a half pound of butter was blended with two cups of sugar. Two eggs and one large grated sweet potato, about three cups of flour along with one tablespoon each of cloves, allspice, and cinnamon were mixed in. This mixture was baked in thin layers, stacked, and served with cream. Thanks to great-great-grandmother for many a good meal!

Note: Do not pick persimmons until after a good hard frost or they'll pucker your mouth into a pucker that you could be wearing till spring.

Lucy's Better Butter

Now a family get-together on Carpenter Mountain wouldn't have been complete without one of Lucy's butter-making sessions. After all the adults had wandered off to take care of any nightly chores before bedding down, Lucy gathered all the grandchildren in the kitchen to take turns at the churn. After washing the dasher in hot water, Lucy removed the white cloth covering the clabbered milk and inserted the long pole, with the wooden cross bars on the end, through the hole in the lid of the churn. Just any old dasher wouldn't do for Lucy. Holman spent many hours hewing her butter-making equipment from hickory wood he'd cut for that purpose.

Churning was a tedious job. The chore was made lighter by many hands and the singing of rhymes as they beat the cream that had been skimmed from the milk and stored until it soured. Little hands, wanting to lift the lid to see if the soft yellow balls had begun to form, slowed the process. After a while, Hattie's young-un, impatient to taste the fresh buttermilk that would be left after the butter was skimmed from the top, stomped her foot and demanded that Lucy finish the churning because she made better butter. Hence, the butter at the Carpenter house became known as Lucy's Better Butter.

After the butter gathered in clusters, it was skimmed from the buttermilk and placed in a bowl. Here it was washed in cold water until all the milk was removed. Salting, kneading, and then molding in a wooden mold with a design on the bottom finished the job. The butter and buttermilk were stored in the nearby springhouse until needed.

To try butter making, place some whipping cream in a jar and cover tightly. Shake until small yellow balls form and gather in a cluster. Remove and wash all the milk away using cold water. Put it in candy molds to make it pretty or just store it covered in the refrigerator. It won't be as good as Lucy's Better Butter because you didn't have to work as hard to make it, but it will be a sample of the way life used to be.

Apple Butter

What would fall be without a good batch of Lucy's apple butter? After the children gathered the winesaps that grew in the Carpenter orchard, Lucy would sort out the sound ones to be stored for eating in the dead of winter, the ones for drying or bleaching, and the leftovers she'd make into apple butter. She'd add four cups of sugar, one quarter cup of vinegar, and lots of cinnamon to about a gallon of cooked apples. This was cooked in the oven until thick enough to slice when it was cold. It made great eating with Lucy's Better Butter and cathead biscuits.

Flap Jacks

Sometimes when Lucy had a fire in the cook stove, she'd fry a thin cornmeal mixture. This was made from her home-grown corn, ground at the Hastings gristmill, with salt, soda, buttermilk, and bacon grease. She'd flip them over, browning them on both sides. These were eaten with sorghum and butter. Today we use them like a soft taco shell, putting on our seasoned hamburger, refried beans, chopped onion, sour cream, lettuce and tomato, and top with shredded cheese. They can't be picked up and eaten, but for something so good, we can wash a plate and fork. Use two cups of cornmeal mix, a quarter cup of oil, and one egg with enough buttermilk to make the consistency of pancake batter.

Pickled Beans and Corn

Lucy pickled a lot of the produce gathered from her garden: corn, beets, green tomatoes, and beans. Holman wasn't much on pickles, but Lucy's pickled beans and corn were pretty good eating in the dead of winter.

Lucy would sit rocking on the front porch stringing the beans while the little-uns sat around the big old dishpan breaking them. Later, she'd wash them until they were squeaky-clean, and cook until tender. Then she'd start in on the field corn, shucking and shelling it, then cooking it as well. After they were mixed, she'd pack them into a crock, cover with water, and add plenty of salt. When the salty brine covered the top of the beans, she'd weigh the whole thing down with a smooth rock from the creek. They'd sit for a week to ten days or until they got sour enough, then she'd take them out and preserve them in jars.

To serve the pickled beans and corn: open, drain off the liquid and simmer in bacon grease until hot. Serve as a vegetable. Cabbage (sauerkraut) and green tomatoes can be pickled the same way.

School Lunches

Our father, Koyle, loved to tell about the boy in his class who never brought a dinner. One day the teacher asked, "Troy, why don't you bring your dinner?"

He looked her in the eye and said, "Teach, did you ever try to carry gravy in a poke?"

Lucy's crew carried their dinner to school or work in a lard bucket. Sacks, bags, or pokes as they called them, were very hard to come by. If they had a sack, it was a flour sack or feed sack and those were used for making into clothes. By the time the grand-young-uns and great grand-young-uns came along, pokes were used, but they were brought home every day for the return trip the next day.

In Lucy's time, dinner would more than likely be a chunk of cornbread from supper the night before and a jar of syrup. If it was the right time of year there might be fresh fruit. Sometimes there were cold biscuits with leftover meat inside.

Today, lunch is cooked at school and many children purchase it rather than bringing their own. If they decide to pack, they need to make sure they have a balanced meal consisting of a sandwich, a few raw vegetables, a piece of fruit, and something sweet.

Have we come a long way? Today's children think biscuits are great and will trade their bought lunch for one. Things do come full circle.

Sweets and Such

On one of the rare trips into town when I was about six or seven, I remember getting my first ice cream cone. It was bought at the soda fountain of a drugstore. I'd never tasted anything so good. Too bad I didn't get to eat it.

Our ride home was either in a taxi or a neighbor's car. All I can remember about the car was that the doors opened backward instead of forward and that my mother was determined that we didn't make a mess in it. Once in the car with the ice cream cone, I decided that I wanted to taste the cone part. Holding it up in the air, I bit off the bottom. It didn't take long for the ice cream to start dripping. My mother made me throw it out the window. I swore then that when I got big I'd live on ice cream. Well, just like everything else, ice cream isn't as good as it used to be. In fact, I don't care that much for it.

—Eva

Birthday Ice Cream

It wasn't only the celebration of Holman's birthday on July third that the children of the mountain looked forward to. It was the one time of the year that they had homemade ice cream. Martha's husband, Lester, would make a special trip back into town in the late afternoon and bring out a block of ice while Lucy stirred up the fixin's for the ice cream.

She'd send some of the grand-young-uns to the springhouse to collect the batch of cream she'd stored especially for this event, along with a jug of fresh sweet milk.

51

By the time they returned, she had the fire burning in the stove and the pan ready. She'd let one grand-young-un measure three cups of the heavy cream while another poured in one-and-a-half cups of sweet milk. Lucy added two teaspoons of pure vanilla to the cream mixture and put it on the stove to bring to a simmer.

Then she broke six eggs into a bowl. Every child begged to help crack the eggs, but she knew all too well how much Holman hated to bite into eggshells. While she whisked the eggs, she allowed a child to pour in a cup of sugar, then she blended this into the hot cream mixture. A bigger child was allowed to stir the sauce over medium-low heat until the custard thickened. To get medium-low heat on a wood cook stove, the pan is set farther away from the wood box. It was thick enough when it left a path on the back of the spoon or when a finger was drawn across it, and it took about six minutes. Lucy was careful not to let it boil.

When Lucy was satisfied with the thickness of the custard, she'd strain it into a large bowl and stir in fruit, which this time of year was blackberries, raspberries, or peaches. Someone would take the bowl outside to Lester, while Lucy and company would stir up another batch. It took at least four gallons for each person to have a taste.

Outside, Lester put the custard into a hand-cranked ice cream maker and packed the ice around it, sprinkling generously with course salt. Everyone took turns cranking. The whole process took time, but the end results were well worth the work and waiting.

Blackberry Pie

Lucy believed that if there were berries to be picked, they were picked. So from early July to mid-August, the young-uns picked berries . . . and picked berries . . . and picked berries. They picked until their hands were first pink, then purple, then a dark, dark, purplish-black from the berry juice. There were pots, pans, and baskets full of berries. These were canned whole, juiced, or used to make jellies and jams.

Nannie's favorite was Lucy's blackberry pie. Every time she'd come in and find Lucy making pie, she'd dance and sing "Four and twenty blackbirds baked in a pie . . ." Then she'd flounce down on the bench behind the table and wait. She always wanted to be the first one for pie. One time Nannie came home before the others, arriving just as Lucy removed her pie from the oven. When Lucy left the room, Nannie proceeded to eat the whole thing. Actually, that was the last time Nannie asked for blackberry pie! Hmmm . . .

Lucy made the pie by picking out the juiciest, ripest berries and layering the bottom of a big pan. She added water just to the top of the berries, a little sugar, and strips of biscuit dough. Then she repeated all the layers, criss-crossing the final layer of biscuit dough, ending with a little extra sugar on top of the last layer of dough. She baked this in a hot oven until brown and bubbly.

Black Walnut Cake

That old walnut tree out by the barn shaded many a family picnic, held the swing for all the Carpenter young-uns, and is still standing even though the barn is gone. The family prized the sweet meat of the black walnut, but the process of getting the meat was tedious. As soon as the green-hulled walnuts started hitting the ground, the young-uns were out picking them up and hulling 'em. They had to remove the hull and extract the hard black nut from the walnut-colored muck inside. The Carpenter young-uns were not alone in attending school in the fall with hands the color of furniture.

The walnuts were put out to dry. Late into the evenings, Lucy cracked open the hard-shelled wonders. She sat in front of the fire with two flat irons. One she held between her knees, placing the walnut on the smooth, flat surface, and whacking it with the other iron. Then, she painstakingly extracted each little broken piece of meat from the crevices. When she came upon a particularly stubborn piece, she'd reach into her bun and pull out a hairpin. The rounded end was perfect for scooping the tasty morsels from the tiny crevices.

Of course, hulling, drying, and cracking walnuts takes a good amount of time, and Lucy wasn't much on helping those who could help themselves. The rest of the family joined in, although not necessarily in the way Lucy found helpful. When she thought she had just about enough for a cake, Mary would dart in and grab a big handful, then race off into the kitchen. The other young-uns tagged along behind, and they'd giggle and whisper as they salted and ate the nuts. In a few minutes, they were peeking back through the door to see if there were more to steal!

This is how Lucy would make her famous black walnut cake. First, she would stir up her favorite yellow cake recipe. She'd put a good heaping cup of walnut meat into a clean cloth and beat with a hammer until finely ground, then add it to the cake batter. Once the cake was baked and frosted, she'd sprinkle more walnuts pieces over the frosting.

For frosting, Lucy whipped egg whites with a fork until frothy, then beat in about a half cup of sugar syrup. The syrup was poured slowly into the frothy egg whites which she continued to beat until the frosting was thick and fluffy. To make sugar syrup, she combined one-and-a-half cups of sugar, two teaspoons of light corn syrup, one-third cup of cold water, and a dash of salt. She would add a teaspoon of vanilla if she had it. The sugar mixture was cooked until a small amount formed a soft ball when dropped into water.

Here is the secret of cracking walnuts to get the meat out in big pieces. Hold the nut between the thumb and forefinger with the pointed end up and hit it with a hammer. It splits in quarters and the meat is easy to remove.

Emmer's Chess Pie

The Sunday Emmer showed up with pie at the church homecoming was the day Martha decided she was going to grow up and be just like Emmer because she wanted to bake pies like hers. This is the story of how Emmer's chess pie became known as Emmer's chest pie.

Martha stood quietly by listening to Emmer tell Lucy how she'd created this pie. "I started out with one-and-a-half cups of sugar, then added a half cup of butter." She hesitated, looked around and whispered, "I whipped the devil out of the sugar and butter, then added one tablespoon of cornmeal and some cream from my churn. A small teaspoon of vinegar will help blend the cornmeal taste and it'll take three egg yolks to thicken it. Since I've gotten a new bottle of vanilla extract, not that imitation stuff, I dropped in a couple of capfuls."

Turning to set out her platter of fried chicken, she said, "Don't forget to bake for about an hour at medium heat, and make it in time for it to set for a couple of hours before serving." She dug another pie from the box. "I think my ma used to call them chess pies. Course, I don't guess mine will be as good as hers because my memory is failing me."

Martha didn't move an inch until Emmer went to put her box back in the wagon, then she crept up to Lucy. "Ma, them are the prettiest pies I ever saw. Can I make one of Emmer's chest pies tonight?"

Lucy wrapped an arm around Martha's shoulder. "If we can find enough eggs I think that would be nice, but honey, they're not chest pies. They're called chess pies."

"No, Ma, they're not. Look, Emmer is wearing part of them across her chest and I'm making one nice and big just like Emmer's chest."

Gingerbread

Lucy didn't really make gingerbread, but her neighbor Bessie did. Lucy generally timed her visits to Bessie's to coincide with baking day. The sweet, spicy aroma of the ginger would waft out the door as Lucy entered Bessie's kitchen.

Bessie's gingerbread: Sift a couple of handfuls of flour, a teaspoon of baking soda, and a little salt together. Add equal amounts of ginger and cinnamon and a little brown sugar. Add one egg and a good dollop of molasses, then only enough liquid to mix smooth. Pour into a pan and bake in a moderately hot oven until done. Serve with cold fruit (applesauce). Bessie always had what she called a "spare pan" to send home with Lucy.

Grapes in a Crock

Most people say spring is their favorite time of year. New life is bursting forth from every crack and crevice of the earth. The smell of freshly turned soil tinges the air with a damp, sweet dirt scent. Even the animals sense the need to replenish and the barnyards began to fill with young life.

This is a picture that is hard to beat, but for many folks there's no prettier time than fall. The mountains are blazing with orange, yellow, brown, and red colors. Fields stand ready to harvest as heads of wheat wave in the breeze. Corn tassels turn brown, telling us that the corn is ready to pull.

Children, enjoying the last of the warmth by splashing bare-foot in the creek, give the feeling of a job well done.

One clear memory of fall in the mountains is the smell of fox grapes. Lucy would take us to the woods hunting the precious fruit. Long before the vines were found, climbing and wrapping their way toward the top of trees, the sweet grape smell tickled our noses. The race was on to see who could find and pick the most.

When they were gathered, Lucy took them home, washed them, and packed them in one of her crocks. Then she heated enough molasses to cover. To seal, she dipped a cloth in hot beeswax and tied it over the crock. Then she took another cloth, dipped it in hot tallow, and tied it over the beeswax wrap. One of the boys took the crock out to the cellar for her. She'd stand guard until cold weather. By then the fruit was slightly fermented, and we were free to fill our waiting bellies. Now we realize why we felt lightheaded after a bite of her molasses grapes.

Fruit

Fruit at the Carpenter house referred to the cooked, mashed, winesap apples that Lucy always harvested in the fall. Or rather, Lucy sent the young-uns out to gather them up as they fell from the trees. She and the girls would peel apples for days. Lucy boiled the apples to can, and she also boiled the peelings to extract the juice to make into apple jelly.

Sometimes Lucy added a little sugar to the fruit mixture as she ladled it into the jars, but sometimes she didn't. Holman and the young-uns never knew which they had when they opened a jar of Lucy's fruit. So they just puckered up to be prepared. If the fruit didn't turn out sweet, they could always just kiss Lucy instead!

Plugged Watermelon

To know anything at all about the South is to know there's no other food that Southerners like better than watermelon. The mountain people are no exception, especially Holman's boys. One favorite pastime was stealing watermelons from a neighbor. One man would always plant a few extra for "the boys," as he called them. When the boys found this out, they'd steal from another neighbor and float them down the creek to put them in the other man's patch. He'd get pure joy out of telling folks what a good crop he'd had since he planted some for "the boys."

After a raid, they'd bring home two or three to plant in the nearby branch to get good and cold. As soon as Holman saw them, he'd take out his pocketknife, cut a good-sized plug from one end, and add a fair amount of his Cherries Jubilee. When it was time to cut the melons, he'd make sure that the menfolk got the plugged melon and before the evening was over, they were feeling mighty fine.

Sweet Bread

This easy treat was always a favorite in the Carpenter household. Lucy would simply throw a cup of flour, a dash of baking powder, a touch of salt, a cup of sugar, a cup of buttermilk, and one egg in a bowl and stir it up well. This was poured into a cake pan and baked in a moderate oven. The bowl was passed to Baby Martha, but if Lucy didn't keep an eye out, she'd find Martha had more help than she wanted with licking the sweet dough.

Cathead Pie Dough

Lucy would never spend half a day trying out pie recipes. Pies usually only happened when there was something left over from supper the night before. Sometimes when the winesaps were in season, she could be talked into making an apple pie.

To make the crust, be it pies or cobblers, she'd make an extra blob of her cathead biscuit dough and squeeze off enough to make the crust. Flouring a piece of a white feed sack that she used for rolling out crust, noodles, and her Sunday rolls, she'd squash the dough flat with the rolling pin that Holman had made her from a hickory log.

Rolling the dough until it was paper-thin, Lucy put it in any pan it would fit into and filled it with whatever filling she had on hand. If there wasn't enough of one kind, well, there wasn't much wrong in mixing two kinds. It all goes to the same place anyway.

Sweet Potato Pie

Using leftover biscuit dough for piecrust, Lucy would scoop out the meat from leftover baked sweet potatoes. A cup of sugar was added, mostly because that was all she could afford to waste on something as frivolous as pie. Sometimes if there was brown sugar, a little was added. If it had been a good churning day and there was plenty of butter, she'd add about a half cup of butter and always a dab for extra measure. If she was short on butter, then a few spoons of heavy cream had to do. Three or four egg yolks were added to make it nice and thick. Spices such as nutmeg and cinnamon can be added, but Lucy usually didn't have many exotic spices, especially after Jake, the peddler, quit making his rounds. It never failed that Hattie would remind her that it would have tasted better with some of the peddler's cinnamon.

Thanksgiving Pumpkin Pie

Nothing went to waste in Lucy's house, and even the Halloween pumpkin had more than one use. Lucy cooked it up and canned it for Thanksgiving. She rolled out biscuit dough for pie crust and filled it with canned pumpkin that she'd already seasoned with a half teaspoon salt, a half teaspoon cinnamon, a quarter teaspoon each ginger, ground cloves, and nutmeg. To this she'd add a half cup of heavy cream and three yolks. She'd then beat the three egg whites nice and stiff and fold them into the pumpkin mixture. It was baked in the wood stove until a broom straw was stuck in and came out clean. These were always made the day before so they'd have time to firm up.

Molasses Candy

One sure sign that fall had come was when the wagons lumbered up the rutted lane toward Holman's syrup mill. Not too far behind came a string of children, hoping for a chance to feed the cane into the giant rollers that squashed out the juice from the cane. Or better yet, a little of the sweet liquid to drink, not realizing that too much would give them "the trots."

The molasses candy that was made from the last run of syrup was something that attracted adults as well as children. Holman would let it cook until it was thick, adding a little soda to keep down the foaming. When it was good and stiff, it was divided out into portions and the people would couple up, grease their hands, and pull the candy back and forth until it was brittle.

It was broken into pieces for easy eating during the square dance that followed or evenings spent around the fireplace come cold weather.

Dried Apple Stack Cake

The Carpenter young-uns knew the pot of soaking dried apples meant that Lucy intended to make a dried apple stack cake. That suspicion was confirmed when she pulled out a large mixing bowl and began to let the young-uns dump in ingredients. Emily was allowed to shovel in about four cups of flour. Mary packed a cup full of brown sugar and poured it in. Lou Ellen spooned out a tablespoon of ginger, one-half teaspoon baking powder, about two teaspoons of baking soda, a half teaspoon of salt, and added these to the dry ingredients. Lucy took care of cracking the eggs and adding them because eggshells weren't too easy to digest. Little Martha was allowed to dump in a third of a cup of Holman's sorghum molasses, a half cup shortening, and two table-spoons of buttermilk after Lucy had measured them.

After all hands were washed, they were allowed to mix the batter with their hands until they had a stiff dough. This dough was placed in the cellar overnight to get cold. The next day the dough was worked with flour until it was stiff enough to roll out like cookie dough and cut. It was cut with a plate or pot lid and baked in a hot oven for five minutes or until done.

Lucy usually had about four or five thin layers. She'd stack them on a plate and smear the cooked dried apples, flavored with a little cinnamon and sugar, between the layers. She'd let this sit overnight so the apples would soften the cake layers. Three days to make a cake that would disappear at one setting! Of course, if Lucy had enough ingredients she'd double the recipe, since it took so long.

Wild Blackberry Jelly

Nothing drips from a hot biscuit on a cold morning like a dollop of freshly churned butter drenched in wild black-berry jelly. The young-uns sure did love it, but they weren't quite as fond of all the work that went into creating the scrumptious treat. If it was a warm spring, the blackberries began to ripen in July. Although they needed lots of rain to grow plump and juicy, the Dog Days afternoon thunderstorms required Lucy to be up and out in the briars fairly early to harvest the berries before the heavy rains washed them away. The berry picking itself was not really dangerous, but she did have to watch out for the black bears, who loved the berries as much as her young-uns loved the jelly, and also for the snakes, who loved to sun themselves on the white quartz rocks that dotted the pastures. Lucy usually tried to take one of the boys with her, but one mid-July morning all the children had escaped except Nannie who was following her around chattering like a magpie, as usual. Lucy loved Nannie but she swore the child would talk to a milepost just to hear the sound of her own voice!

So, Lucy and Nannie set off for the berry patch. Nannie kept up a running dialogue, her mouth moving faster than her feet. When Lucy stopped to pick the newly ripened berries by the branch, Nannie jumped atop a large rock and continued her oration for all the world to hear. Lucy plucked all the berries she could reach, then turned to motion Nannie to follow. There was Nannie on top of the rock, rattling on for all she was worth. And there, sunning himself on the warm rock, was the biggest copperhead Lucy had ever seen. His beady eyes were fixed on the girl on the rock and his thin, forked tongue darted in and out as if he were licking his lips in anticipation of a delicious meal.

Startled, Lucy screamed and dropped her bucket. Nannie's eyes focused on Lucy's face, then followed the trail of tumbling bucket and spilling berries right up to the bottom of her rock, and the copperhead. Without really thinking at all, Nannie catapulted over the snake and into Lucy's arms. The snake, now desperate to flee the scene, started to squeeze back under the rock. But Lucy never went berry picking unprepared, and she brought the sharp edge of her garden hoe down across his neck, separating his pointed head from the rest of his squirming body.

From that day on, one of the boys was always waiting to accompany Lucy berry picking. Strangely enough, Nannie had lost her zeal to talk to the world and kept her eyes firmly on where she was placing her feet when she went out into the pastures.

To make Wild Blackberry Jelly, carefully wash the plumpest, ripest berries, then boil in fresh spring water. Mash up the berries as they cook, then strain the juice through several layers of clean cheesecloth. Bring eight cups of blackberry juice and one package of pectin to a full boil. Let boil one minute. Gradually add nine cups of granulated sugar, stirring constantly. Return to a full boil and cook until the juice begins to gather on the spoon when allowed to drip. Pour into hot, just-washed jelly glasses, cover with beeswax, and let cool.

Teas, Herbs, and Medicinals

Mountain people are a prideful people, proud to be able to take care of their own. Doctors were sometimes used for birthing and later for dying, but Lucy learned lessons from her mother and tended her flock as she was taught to do. Even as late as the "War on Poverty" years, I remember my own mother dosing us with some of Lucy's remedies, my older sister smoking a foul-smelling cigar rolled from rabbit tobacco for her toothache, and my brother-in-law drinking catnip tea to soothe his nerves after a particularly harrowing cut that almost severed his hand from his arm. After living this, believe me, an HMO is a wonderful improvement!

—Emma

Forget-me-nots

The rooster crowed and Lucy's feet hit the floor. Whoever was milking this morning would have already stoked the fire burning in the old cook stove. What would today bring? The only thing she could plan on being the same each day was fixing food for the family. Cooking three meals a day sure kept a body busy.

As soon as breakfast dishes were done, preparation for the noon dinner would have to be under way. She knew that the menfolk would come in from the field starving. At least supper wouldn't be too hard—just another pan of cornbread to go along with the leftovers from dinner. If there weren't many leftovers, then cornbread and sweet milk would be supper.

Before breakfast was over, Lucy knew what lay ahead. Harley came to the table scratching like a hound dog with fleas. Of all the young-uns he was the one who was forever getting into poison ivy.

When they were alone, Harley confessed he'd been the one up on the mountain the day before, screaming like a panther. He hadn't planned on his pa getting together a bunch of men to hunt down the vicious cat. When the pack of cat-hungry dogs charged up the mountain, he'd rolled off the log he was sitting on. The dogs, not interested in his human scent, leaped over the log and disappeared up the mountain. He'd found himself lying in a bed of poison ivy leaves. He told Lucy he'd headed to the creek and took a cold dip, hoping to wash away the juice.

She handed him a bar of lye soap and told him to scrub down with the soap and hot water. Lots of hot water with salt would keep down the itching until she found some forget-me-nots. Their juice would cure the water-filled blisters. Forget-me-nots always grew near poison ivy and she knew exactly where to find some.

Ginseng Tea

This root is used mainly for its cool, calming effect, especially for the stomach. After a long day of running her busy household and dealing with Hattie's pranks, Lucy would sit in front of the fire warming her feet and sipping her ginseng tea. She spent days hunting the forest for the bright red berries on this low-growing plant, then digging the roots for her bag. She carried home the treasure, washed the roots, and laid them by the fire to dry. What she didn't use for herself and her family, she sent to town with Holman to sell. This meager pittance helped buy the coffee they used through the long winter months.

Roots are generally dried to sell or make tea. Steep them in a teapot of boiling water to desired strength.

Snakeroot Tea

Lucy learned about healing herbs at her mother's knee, but Dovey was right to be concerned about the snakeroot tea. If Lucy had mistakenly pulled the deadly White Snakeroot instead of Virginia Snakeroot, baby Martha would have been dead within a matter of hours. Lucy would have been wishing she'd declined the cow's offer of her tail to escape the sinkhole.

If you are sure you've picked the right snakeroot, wash the root well and boil to make a weak tea, about one teaspoon dried root in one cup of water. Drain off the broth and sweeten with honey to give it good flavor. Use as needed for fever.

Clover Tea

The one ingredient for making tea that didn't have to be searched for in the mountains was clover. It grew in abundance in pastures and along fencerows. Sometimes it would grow in neighbors' yards, but most yards were neatly swept red clay. Lucy made sure she picked plenty of the full-grown leaves and blossoms and dried them in the summer sun. When they were shriveled up and brown, she'd rub them into small pieces and store in a tightly covered jar. When the cold mountain winds howled, she'd brew a cup in boiling water and sweeten with a little honey. This was a tea she could always have on hand because it was so easy to gather. It was also used when any of the young-uns would come down with a coughing fit.

Holman's White Lightning

While Lucy enjoyed her quiet respite with a cup of ginseng tea, Holman firmly believed in the medicinal value of a tablespoon of whiskey every night before bed. In his early years, he distilled his own, but when he went to work for the government, his 'shinin' days were over. He thought that a pity, too. Not only because he made the best moonshine in the county, but he didn't have anything to keep the feud between him and Mr. Byrd going. He just couldn't stand it when that little man came prancing around bragging about what a good run he'd had that year!

Here's how Holman made his whiskey. Every year he would carry some of his best field corn down to the mill and have Joe Hastings grind it on his water-powered gristmill. He would barter for the service, either a full measure of corn, or a gallon or two of the finished product. When he came home with his freshly ground meal, he'd carry Lucy's big, black, three-legged pot down to the spring. He needed plenty of the sweet spring water to mix up the cornmeal, water, sugar, and yeast. He let this sit until it fermented, then he boiled the mash and caught the vapor using copper tubes or pipes and let this condense again into liquid and drip into a clean pot. The end result was a liquid as clear as the spring water that would take the hide off'n a dead skunk!

Cherries Jubilee

Making white lightning wasn't the only skill Holman had. Lucy didn't have anything on him when it came to spicing up his already perfected moonshine recipe. As soon as the last drop of homemade liquor was bottled, he'd store away a gallon for later use. When the cherries (wild or tame) were ripe, many a neighbor reported seeing Holman fighting the birds for the precious fruit. He'd manage to save a couple of gallon pails. First, he'd dump them in cold spring water and wait for the worms to float to the top. Once the worms were skimmed off, he'd put the cherries in one of the churns he'd been able to con out of Lucy. He'd add the same amount of spring water as he had cherries, and hope no more worms floated to the top. If they did, he'd pretend he didn't see them and dump in a five-pound bag of white sugar. He'd mash sugar and berries together (plus any leftover worms) and a gallon of his white lightning. This mixture needed to sit for about four months and be stirred from time to time with a wooden spoon. At the end of four months, he'd strain out the seeds and pulp and pour the liquid into jars, seal, and let sit for a few more weeks. When the cold wind howled around their old house, he'd pull out a jar and dole out no more than an ounce to each member of his family old enough to partake. The licking of lips and jubilant smiles of contentment were reward enough for him.

When asked where the recipe originated, Holman didn't have to be prompted to tell how some of his forefathers had been from France and brought it with them when they set out to make their fortune trapping furs in the wilderness of the Great Smoky Mountains.

Home Brew

Holman's boys liked home brew better than their pa's moonshine. When they got their hands on some store-bought malt and yeast, they'd borrow one of Lucy's crocks (without her knowledge), and head off to a secluded place in the woods to stir up a batch. They'd build a fire and heat a gallon and a half of water in the crock. Next, they'd dump in a five-pound bag of sugar, a quart of Red Top Malt, and stir until dissolved. Three-and-a-half gallons of fresh spring water were poured in, cooling the mixture until "milk warm," then two cakes of yeast were added. In about three days, after foaming and settling down, it would be ready to bottle or can.

The boys never suspected that Lucy and Holman knew what they'd been up to when they came home a little tipsy.

Parsnip Wine

When Holman planted parsnips, he always said he was planting them for hog feed. In his book, hogs were about the only thing that should be eating this turnip-like bulb. What he never told anyone was how much he liked a glass of parsnip wine. In the middle of February, he'd harvest a bundle and when Lucy wasn't around, he'd grate them up and let them sit on the back of the stove in a gallon of hot water for about four hours without boiling. He'd then strain and add about three pounds of sugar and stir until dissolved. When this mixture cooled, he'd add one quarter cup of liquid yeast. He'd tuck it away in the cellar until it seasoned and when he'd pass by he'd take a little nip, reasoning it helped his rheumatism.

Lye Soap

Another fact of life with seventeen kids was lice infestation. But the lice didn't have time to infest at Lucy's house. At the first sign of trouble, Lucy grabbed a bar of her homemade lye soap and started scrubbing. She scrubbed each child meticulously from head to toe, while boiling all the clothes and bedclothes in more of the bubbling lye concoction. Pity the poor child who carried the first nit home! Lucy scrubbed that one twice, then shaved his head and scrubbed him all over again.

Lucy made her soap in the fall, after the lye leeching, hog killing, and lard rendering. And after the hog killing and lard rendering, there really wasn't much to making soap except dumping the lard and lye into her black pot and stirring and standing, and standing and stirring. She only let the older young-uns help with the soap making because the lye would burn, mightily, if they got it on them. But basically she preferred just to do it herself. If she were feeling especially motherly toward the girls, she'd throw in some extract from roses or lilacs toward the end. Her preference was the wild pear blossoms that grew down by the branch. Holman liked that one too, especially when she washed her hair in it.

Sulphur and Molasses

Every spring about the time the wild violets started to bloom, Lucy sent Holman into town for the sulphur. Her mother always gave her sulphur and molasses for spring fever, and she continued the tradition with the young-uns. Truth be told, Lucy wasn't quite sure what spring fever was, but she believed it was better to be safe than sorry, and if her mother did it, then so would she.

She'd dump a handful of the sulphur into a quart of the homemade molasses saved from last fall's syrup making. Then she sat all the victims she could find around the big supper table and ladled a heaping tablespoon into their squirreled-up mouths. If any of the young-uns looked especially peaked, she'd dose them twice. It wasn't long before there was a line forming by the outhouse, and if Hattie took too long, some of the boys trotted off into the woods to relieve their pain, hence the term "the trots."

Turpentine for Worms

Lucy just couldn't stand worms, and the only sure cure she knew of was a few drops of turpentine in a teaspoon of sugar. She hated to waste her good white sugar on those worms, but there just wasn't any other way to get the turpentine down the young-uns! So at the first grumble of a stomachache, out would come the turpentine and sugar. For an extra measure of protection, a few drops of the strong-smelling turpentine were rubbed around the navel.

Sunday Dinner

I can describe Sunday dinner with one dish: banana pudding. Homemade banana pudding. Of course it wasn't every Sunday that we were offered this treat; but when times were good, Daddy would bring home a small bunch of this tropical fruit on Saturday and magically they were transformed into a smooth, rich dessert. The amazing thing was that just a few bananas could feed all the family, visitors, and neighbors. It sort of reminds me of Jesus feeding the five thousand with only five loaves and two fishes. But, unlike that miracle, there were no leftovers. I distinctly remember scraping the sides of the serving bowl with my spoon to glean the last, sweet taste.

—Emma

Martha awoke early on Sunday morning. At first she couldn't figure out why, but then she heard a "cock-a-doodle-doo" coming from the barn. To her surprise, this was followed by an immediate commotion in the kitchen. She heard Lucy's voice rise above the others as she said, "a whistling woman and a crowing hen will always come to some bad end. Harley, go on up to the barn and bring me that pullet. I was gonna make fried chicken today anyway. The District Superintendent is coming today and you know how your Daddy loves to bring company home for dinner."

Harley groaned and Martha heard the door slam as he headed off to do Lucy's bidding. Martha snuggled deeper into the featherbed and pondered why whistling women always came to some bad end. She didn't think too hard about the chicken because Lucy's Sunday dinners were renowned throughout the mountains. Why, the District Superintendent of the Methodist Conference was coming all the way from Tennessee! Since Daddy had become a regular attendee and Sunday School teacher for the new Methodist church, he made sure visiting dignitaries had a proper meal under their belts before they started the preaching, converting, and baptizing. But at eight years old, Martha was sure that the real reason so many people crowded around the big kitchen table on Sundays was more Lucy's cooking than Holman's praying.

Martha hopped out of bed, dressed quickly, and hurried off to help get her new little brothers ready for church. Koyle especially liked to be there in time for the singing. All the while Martha's mouth watered as she dwelt on Sunday dinner: fried chicken, mashed taters and gravy, roasted corn still on the cob, and green beans. Of course dinner included the Anadama rolls and apple pies Lucy baked on Saturday. And to drink, why, some of Martha's own buttermilk she'd hand-churned while Lucy baked. The pies, buttermilk, and butter were even now cooling in the springhouse.

Southern Fried Chicken, Lucy-style

First, just any old chicken would not do. To have fried chicken, Lucy started with young fryers. From the time the baby chicks peeked from the shell, she decided how many roosters were needed to keep her flock multiplying. She rarely cooked a pullet (that's a young hen) as long as there was a rooster left to fry. As soon as the chicks lost that soft fuzz and grew feathers, she'd scoop up a few and wring their necks. For reasons unknown to the family, she never chopped off their heads like she did the roosters. I've often wondered if it was because she felt they deserved an easier death than the old mean roosters. Anyway, dead is dead, and bleeding is bleeding, and bleeding is what happened when the head was gone. Lucy would cut off their heads after they were dead, and the chicken was always hung, head down, until the blood had dripped out.

As the last drop of blood hit the ground, Lucy would plunge the fryer into a boiling pot of water, pluck off the feathers, then singe off the fine hair. She quickly found the joints and snapped them so the knife would slide through, easily cutting breasts, thighs, drumsticks and wings into frying pieces. Lucy would fry the whole thing, including backs, necks, and livers. She especially loved the crispy livers and sometimes snuck them out of the pan before they made it to the platter!

Lucy melted some lard from the last rendering into big iron skillets. Then she beat an egg or two into buttermilk while the girls mixed some salt and fresh herbs from her garden into a bowl of flour. When the pans were hot enough, Lucy rolled the chicken pieces in the flour mixture, then dipped them into the buttermilk. If necessary, she'd dust with flour again and pop into the pan. The coated pieces of meat were added, covered with a heavy lid, and pushed away from the hottest part of the stove. When one side of the chicken browned to a golden color, the pieces were turned and browned on the other side. When they were ready to serve, the pieces were placed on a platter that was called Lucy's special chicken plate.

Chicken Gravy

Lucy removed the chicken from the frying pans, put it in another pan covered with dish towels, and stuck it in the warming ovens to keep it warm until dinner. She drained the excess fat and set the pans back to stay warm. Right before the company sat down to eat, she liberally sprinkled the remaining chicken drippings with the leftover flour and herb mixture and set the girls to stirring constantly until each pan was browned. She would add enough water to make the flour a soft paste, which helps it maintain its color. Then she would add enough milk to make the gravy the right consistency.

She placed the bowls of gravy randomly down the long table where one would be easily within reach of each guest.

Canned Chicken Fryers

The fryers that didn't get fried for the preacher on Sunday made it to the stew pot. As soon as the meat was removed from the bone, Lucy packed it in jars and cooked the jars in a tub of hot water for about thirty minutes. They were stored away in the can house and when there were no more chickens to kill, it was opened and usually turned into chicken pie. Rolling biscuit dough and putting over the dish of chicken and its broth accomplished this. Vegetables could be added.

Lucy's Special Chicken and Dumplings

One of Lucy's requirements for her chicken and dumplings was a large rooster, preferable a fighting one. This gave her reason to slaughter it without feeling like she was contributing to the demise of her flock of chickens.

Not much time elapsed between when she placed her foot on the rooster's neck, lowered her axe, and he wound up in her stew pot, plucked clean. He was cooked until the meat fell from the bones. This process took the better part of a day. The meat was then removed and the broth was allowed to stand until cool. When the fat had hardened to a thick layer on top, Lucy would scoop it off and add it to a large bowl of flour. When the fat and flour were mixed, she'd add some eggs and enough broth to make stiff dough. The pastry was rolled paper thin and cut into strips. The broth was reheated to a rolling boil, then the strips of pastry dropped into the hot bubbly liquid. After all the noodles were added, the chicken meat was placed back into the pot. When Lucy served chicken and dumplings for Sunday dinner at the Carpenter house, leftovers were not a concern.

Mashed Taters

"'Tain't nothing special, just mashed some taters," Lucy replied as her guests complimented her on Sunday dinner. But those taters were probably the most time-consuming part of the dinner. She had the girls peeling taters a good part of the morning. After they cooked until they fell apart when she stuck them with a fork, she dumped them into her biggest dishpan and gave two of the girls tater mashers to work on getting them smooth. When Martha got back from church with the boys, Lucy sent her to the springhouse to bring up the butter, then dumped two large pats into the taters and the girls stirred it in.

Roast'n Ears

Holman started planting some early corn in the garden and Lucy just loved the sweet young kernels when they were roasted in the hot ashes from last night's fire. She had the older boys pull a dozen or so ears before going to church and early in the morning would pull back the ends of the shucks just enough to tug out the long silks and dump any worms that might be nibbling on the young kernels. Then she wrapped the shucks back around the corn and twisted it tight. The hot coals from last night's fire were still in the fireplace, so she stirred up the ashes and buried the ears of corn close enough for the coals to cook them, but insulated enough so they wouldn't burn. When dinner was almost ready, she yanked the corn from the ashes and carried the pan to the back porch. There she shucked each ear carefully, plucking any remaining silks. She served these roasted ears with mounds of fresh butter and salt. Don't know why we called the ears roast'n ears unless it was because they were picked when they were still tender enough to roast.

Boiled Green Beans

Lucy kept a pot of green beans on the back of the cook stove most of the time. In the summer she used fresh ones. One of the advantages of having so many girls at home was they could share the chore of picking, stringing, and breaking the beans. Today they had a fresh pot that Fannie and Nannie had worked on Saturday while she made bread and Martha paddled the buttermilk. The bugs really attacked her garden this year so she'd assigned Fannie the chore of cutting out all the specks on the beans. Those two worked nearly two hours just to get enough beans for the dinner. But there was nothing to stretch a meal like a pot of beans, and Lord knows, today she almost needed a miracle to feed the multitude! She placed the bean bowls on the table between the platters of chicken and mountains of rolls.

Anadama Rolls

Lucy didn't really care for yeast breads, but sometimes she made these rolls because they included a little cornmeal and molasses. On Saturday, she sifted, stirred, and kneaded, then let the dough rest and rise. Then she punched it down and kneaded it again, then let the dough rest and rise. After doing this several times, she was really wearied of the whole process. Only thinking of the pleasure her family and guests got from these rolls kept her at her task. The smell of the baking rolls drifted through the house and it was all she could do to keep the boys out of them until Sunday dinner. On Sunday morning, she placed the rolls in the warming ovens with the chicken to "knock the cold off," and served them with honey and butter.

To make the rolls, she would bring two cups of water to a boil, then gradually add the cornmeal. She stirred the mixture constantly to break up any lumps, then added two tablespoons of butter, a half cup of molasses, and two teaspoons of salt and set it to one side to cool to lukewarm. Lucy then dissolved two cakes of compressed yeast in about half a cup of warm water and added it to cornmeal mixture. She added enough flour (about seven and a half cups, sifted) to make a stiff dough. She kneaded well and then let it stand in a greased and covered bowl until it had doubled in bulk, then would punch it down, knead it again (just a little), and let it rise until light.

After the dough was light enough, she dumped it onto a floured board, flattened it with her hickory rolling pin until it was about a quarter of an inch to a half an inch thick. She'd cut it into rounds, dip in melted butter and fold over, and then let stand to rise again. When she baked them, she didn't have a timer and the wood cook stove wouldn't always be the same temperature anyway, so she would just cook them until her desired crustiness was reached.

Sunday Apple Pie

Lucy thought the best part of Sunday pie was the crust. Her Sunday apple pies were made just a little differently than the pies she made the rest of the week. She especially loved the thin, crisp crust waffled atop her tart winesap apple slices sweetened with honey and maybe a dash of molasses.

Her recipe for good crust was basically butter, plain flour, and egg. She added just enough water to help stick it together, then rolled it paper-thin before lining her pie pans. Proportionally she used one cup butter to three cups of flour and one egg. Of course, she had a secret ingredient. A dash of nutmeg in the crust added just enough flavor to leave those young-uns wanting another bite.

She'd pile the pie dough high with sliced apples, sift with a handful of flour, slather with butter and honey, and add a dribble of molasses. Then she wove strips of the dough across the top. She brushed the latticework with beaten egg whites and sprinkled with a little white sugar if she had any in the house.

She baked in a moderate oven until the apple liquid bubbled and the crust was brown.

Sittin' Down to Dinner

Lucy made some dishes especially for Sunday dinner, but she also warmed and served any leftovers from the week, along with fresh sliced tomatoes, onions, and fruits in season. She generally served at least two kinds of meat.

By the time the family and guests arrived from church and washed up, her table was laden with food and the aroma wafted out to welcome them to dinner. The adults and older courtin' girls with their beaus sat around the big table to be served first.

The children played outside until it was their turn. The children would replace the adults at the table and clean up any leavings. Unfortunately, this usually meant that the only chicken pieces left were wings, backs, and necks. A lucky few might get drumsticks. As she passed the platter, Lucy quietly lifted a wishbone breast piece off the platter and laid it to one side for Martha.

Rising to refill a bowl, Lucy stood at the end of the table behind Holman and surveyed her world. And it was good.

Conclusion

"Nothing is the way it seemed to be." Oh, this saying is so true. These recipes will never taste like they did when Lucy or our mother made them. The homeplace isn't as big as it used to be, or the mountains as tall. Neither would a trip to town be the way it was when we only got to go a few times a year.

If you deny yourself the things you want now thinking it will taste better, wear better, or look better in the future, take it from us. It won't. Life is for living, now.

Index

Eva Carpenter McCall is a granddaughter of Lucy and Holman Carpenter. She grew up in Franklin, North Carolina, then attended Pfeiffer College near Charlotte. She married George McCall, also of Franklin, and they moved to Flint, Michigan, where George worked for General Motors and Eva became a beautician.

It was only after their three children were grown that Eva actively pursued her love of writing. She attended writing workshops and joined professional writers' groups. After several short stories and inspirational articles were published in magazines, Eva turned to writing about Granny Lucy in her first novel, *Edge of Heaven.* A sequel soon followed: *Children of the Mountain.*

Now retired, the McCalls continue to live in Michigan part of the year and spend the remainder in the North Carolina mountains or visiting their children and grandchildren in Tennessee.

Photo courtesy of Powell/Roach

Emma Carpenter Edsall is the youngest of Lucy's grandchildren. Her earliest memories include being "rocked in a straight chair" on Granny Lucy's lap and listening to stories of Tate City, rattlesnakes, and screaming panthers ("painters," Lucy would have said). As a Toastmaster, Emma often delights her audiences by recalling these tales.

Emma graduated from Franklin High School, and in 1973, from Western Carolina University with a degree in social work. She married Bill Edsall in Cullowhee and they moved to Bill's hometown, Concord, North Carolina. Emma is a software engineer with Enovia Corporation in Charlotte.

Bill and Emma have two children and one grandson. Emma's spare time is mostly devoted to being "Granny" to Matthew. However, she still finds time for worship, friends, and her chihuahuas. Writing is a way of life, as both her career and her avocation include writing technical manuals, test cases, or speeches.

Edge of Heaven

When Lucy Davenport is traded by her father to Holman Carpenter in exchange for a mysterious favor, her simple mountaintop life is abruptly changed. Holman's wife had died giving birth to their thirteenth child, and overnight Lucy, herself only a few years older than the oldest child and still mourning the death of her own mother, faces the challenge of caring for Holman's household. Lucy's Cherokee ancestry hampers her acceptance into the family and community, and the lure of leaving Holman to find her mother's people in Cherokee is in constant conflict with her determination to honor her father's commitment to Holman.

Eva McCall's novel is woven from the stories she was told by her grandmother, the real Lucy Davenport, interlaced with Eva's own enthusiastic appreciation of her land and people. *Edge of Heaven* vividly portrays rural life in Western North Carolina in the late 1890s, when the simple joys of family life were often threatened by illness, poverty, and violence. Whether those forces can be successfully overcome by education, faith, and integrity is the question Lucy faces daily.

Children of the Mountain

Ever since Eva McCall wrote about Lucy Davenport's arranged marriage to Holman Carpenter, readers have been eager to know more about the Carpenter family. Together, Lucy and Holman built a new house on the mountain where they raised four more sons. Now, despite having moved away with families of their own, the children still feel bound to Carpenter Mountain.

In this sequel to *Edge of Heaven*, they return home for Holman's final birthday celebration, then help Lucy cope with widowhood. Jake the peddler reappears with his own offer of solace but with dubious intentions. Family conflicts and uncertainty over the future of her home compel Lucy to return to the edge of heaven, seeking wisdom from the spirits of her mother's people. Ultimately, Lucy must look within to clarify her heart's desires.

Order Historical Images books through your local bookstore or from the publisher:
Bright Mountain Books, 206 Riva Ridge Drive, Fairview, NC 28730.
Call 800-437-3959 for further information or to order by credit card.